How to Deal with Debt Collectors and Win Every Time How To Beat Them at Their Own Game

By

Ernie Braveboy

Get Your Free Copy of

How to be a Real Estate Millionaire

To Get Your Free Copy, Open the Link

https://ebraveboy_3ee2.gr8.com/

INTRODUCTION

I want to thank you and congratulate you for buying the book, *"How to Deal with Debt Collectors and Win Every Time How To Beat Them at Their Own Game"*.

This book has actionable information on how to deal with debt collectors and win every time.

If debt collectors have ever come after you, you understand that debt collection is one of the most frightening experiences ever.

Debt collectors are like predators who are always circling around, waiting for a chance to pounce on their prey. Hence, they will use any tricks and techniques to get you to pay up. Sometimes they will threaten you and at other times, they may harass you and make you uncomfortable, all in the bid to get you to rush off to pay whatever bills they claim you owe.

There are several ways to beat debt collectors at their game. Many of the techniques they use to intimidate you are illegal and even when they use legal strategies, there are legal ways to get them off your back.

This book explores techniques and strategies you can use to get debt collectors off your back, erase your debts, and win against them in court if they decide to sue you. This book is a no-fluff, straight to the point, a systematic guide with proven techniques other debtors have used to beat debt collectors at their own game.

Let us dig in.

Thanks again for buying this book. I hope you enjoy it!

© **Copyright 2018 by Ernie Braveboy - All rights reserved.**

This document is geared towards providing exact and reliable information in regards to the topic and issue covered. The publication is sold with the idea that the publisher is not required to render accounting, officially permitted, or otherwise, qualified services. If advice is necessary, legal or professional, a practiced individual in the profession should be ordered.

- From a Declaration of Principles which was accepted and approved equally by a Committee of the American Bar Association and a Committee of Publishers and Associations.

In no way is it legal to reproduce, duplicate, or transmit any part of this document by either electronic means or in printed format. Recording of this publication is strictly prohibited and any storage of this document is not allowed unless with written permission from the publisher. All rights reserved.

The information provided herein is stated to be truthful and consistent, in that any liability, in terms of inattention or otherwise, by any usage or abuse of any policies, processes, or directions contained within is the solitary and utter responsibility of the recipient reader. Under no circumstances will any legal responsibility or blame be held against the publisher for any reparation, damages, or monetary loss due to the information herein, either directly or indirectly.

Respective authors own all copyrights not held by the publisher.

The information herein is offered for informational purposes solely and is universal as so. The presentation of the information is without a contract or any type of guarantee assurance.

The trademarks that are used are without any consent, and the publication of the trademark is without permission or backing by the trademark owner. All trademarks and brands within this book are for clarifying purposes only and are the owned by the owners themselves, not affiliated with this document.

TABLE OF CONTENTS

Introduction iii

Table of Contents vii

Chapter 1: How Debt Collection Agencies Work 1

    Why Businesses Use Debt Collectors 2

    How Debt Collection Agencies Operate 3

Chapter 2: What Debt Collection Agencies are NOT Allowed to Do 5

    What They Cannot Do 6

    How to Report Debt Collection Agents for Harassment or Unfair Practices 11

Chapter 3: What to Do When a Debt Collector Contacts You 14

    How to Respond to Debt Collection Agents on Phone 15

    Why You Should Record Your Conversations with a Debt Collector 18

    Sample Phone Call Transcript to use with Debt Collectors 20

    How to Respond to Letters or Mails 25

    Sample Letter Asking for More Information from the Debt Collector 29

    Sample Debt Dispute with Cease and Desist Order 33

Sample Cease and Desist Letter (If You Indeed Owe the Debt but Do Not Wish to Pay) 36

Sample Letter Directing a Debt Collector to Continue Communications with Your Lawyer 38

What to Do after a Debt Collector Contacts You 39

How to Investigate a Debt 40

What You Should Never Do When Debt Collectors Contact You 42

Steps to Take If a Debt is True and Valid 43

How to Negotiate with Debt Collectors 44

Chapter 4: How to Beat a Debt Collection Agent in Court 48

How to Start Your Defense in Court 60

Conclusion 62

Chapter 1: How Debt Collection

Agencies Work

The first step towards successfully getting debt collectors off your back is to know whom they really are and how they work.

In most cases, debt collectors are representatives of debt collection agencies. However, some debt collection agencies operate individually. Debt collectors act as intermediaries between debtors and creditors. Their job is to help organizations like banks, credit card companies, car dealerships, student loan issuers, utility companies and other creditors to recover delinquent debts from debtors.

Delinquent debts are debts that are at least 60 days past due. They collect the debts and then remit them to the creditor after deducting their commission, which could range from 25-45% of the recovered debt.

Other types of debt collection agencies act as debt buyers. They purchase debts at a discount after a bidding process. For instance, if you owe a company $2,000, a debt buyer may purchase the debt for about $100 and then from there, they take over the debt fully and begin to pursue the debtor to pay up. If they are lucky enough to get the debtor to pay $2,000 or something close, they will make a profit of around $1,900, which is why they can sometimes be very aggressive.

Sometimes, debt collection agencies will try to negotiate a settlement amount with the debtor and encourage the debtor to pay a lesser amount than owed as a final settlement of the debt. Should the debtor refuse to make payments, debt collection agents may decide to file a lawsuit and get a court injunction that will force the debtor to pay up what they owe.

WHY BUSINESSES USE DEBT COLLECTORS

You must be wondering why your creditors will not come after you themselves but choose to use the services of debt collection agencies or even sell your debts to them instead.

Well, here is why:

1. They can be paid a good portion of the money owed to them from the debt collection agency and thus avoid expensive lawsuits. When businesses use debt collection agents, they can focus on their businesses and avoid the stress and expenses that come with debt collection.

2. Debt collectors are very skilled and efficient at recovering debts. They know the right things to say to get money out of debtors. They also have software and tools that they use to differentiate debtors who cannot pay up because they are in financial distress, and debtors who can afford to pay the debts—debt collectors usually go after the latter category since there is a better chance of getting their money from these set of people.

How Debt Collection Agencies Operate

As soon as they take up the job of recovering debts from you, they scrape up all the details they can find about you and then either call you or send you a letter to inform you about the debt as a way to try to convince you to pay up.

Usually, debt collectors have sophisticated software and tools they use to find information about you including your residential address and your phone numbers. At other times, they may look into your bank accounts and other assets you own to see if you can afford to repay the debts.

If after trying to convince you to pay, you do not pay up, debt collectors will usually pursue two courses of actions:

1: Report to Credit Bureaus

Debt collectors understand that reporting your debts to the credit bureaus will hurt your credit score, which may pose some financial problems for you in the future especially when you need to obtain credit from other businesses, which is why if you refuse to pay up, they report the debt to the credit bureaus.

2: Obtain a Court Judgment

A debt collector cannot force you to pay what you owe so what they do is to take the case to court and obtain a judgment against you. If they succeed in court, the court will grant them the right to garnish your wages, which means legally deducting what you owe from your salary account. The court may also give them permission to place a lien on your assets or force a sale in order to recover the debts.

One of the important things you must know when dealing with debt collectors is your rights as a debtor. There are laws that protect you as a debtor. You can use these laws as tools to get debt collectors off your back.

The next chapter discusses these laws in-depth:

Chapter 2: What Debt Collection Agencies are NOT Allowed to Do

Debt collectors are bound by (and operated under) the FDCPA (Fair Debt Collection Practices Act).

The FDCPA is a federal law that specifies what different debt collectors are allowed to do and what they are not allowed to do as they pursue loan recovery. The United States Federal Government put the law in place to keep debt collection agencies from resorting to desperate, deceptive, and unfair measures to recover debts.

The FDCPA law does not apply to business debts; it only applies to personal or family debts such as utility bills, student loans, medical debts, mortgages, credit card bills, and so on. Another thing you must take note of is that this law only applies to debt collection agencies or debt buyers.

If you owe American Express for instance, and someone who works with AMEX contacts you about your debts, the FDCPA law does not apply to them although the government also expects them to be reasonable with their debt collection procedures too. This law applies to third-party debt collectors whose major business is collecting debts for profits.

WHAT THEY CANNOT DO

The law stipulates that third-party debt collectors cannot:

1: Contact you at an Unusual Time or Place

The law requires debt collectors to respect boundaries: they cannot call you whenever and however they like.

The FDCPA law specifies that debt collectors can only call debtors within the hours of 8 am and 9 pm. This means that they cannot call you before 8 am in the morning or after 9 pm in the evening.

In addition, if a debt collector knows that you cannot receive calls during working hours (you can write them an official letter informing them of this), the law keeps them from calling you while you are at work.

2: Contact You after You Refer them to Your Attorney

Once you have a lawyer and tell the debt collector to talk to your attorney, the law dictates that a debt collector CANNOT communicate with you. All further communications should be with your lawyer instead.

3: Harass You

Under no circumstance should a debt collector harass you whether by letter or over the phone. If they do so, you can report them for harassment and they could get in serious trouble for doing so. Harassment has led to bans of many debt collection agencies.

4: Contact You after You Instruct Them to Stop

You can write a letter to a debt collector instructing them to stop contacting you.

This letter is called a **'cease and desist'** letter and as soon as a debt collector gets the letter, they are no longer allowed to contact you about debt repayments except to inform you that they will be taking legal actions against you like reporting you to the credit bureau or taking you to court.

5: Talk to Other People about the Debt You Owe

The law keeps debt collectors from using embarrassment as a debt collection strategy: it keeps them from talking to your employer about your debts except where there is a court injunction against you.

The law keeps them from talking to friends, family, or anybody else but you about your debts. Similarly, it keeps them from publishing your name if you refuse to pay up.

6: Contact You about Debts That Have Passed the Statute of Limitation

This is something you must pay very keen attention to. As soon as a debt collector contacts you, you must investigate the debt the collection agency is talking about to confirm that it has not passed the statute of limitation.

Typically, a debt collector cannot contact you after a debt has passed a period specified by law. This period differs from one state to another but it is usually between 4 and 7 years.

Confirm the statute of limitation for your state and if the time has lapsed, simply tell the debt collector to stop calling you and they will desist.

7: Lie about What You Owe

Debt collectors should do their due diligence properly before they start contacting you: the Fair Debt Collection Practices Act states that they cannot contact you about debts you do not owe or lie about what you owe.

8: Make False or Bogus Claims or Threats

A debt collector cannot threaten to arrest you or place a lien on your assets except in instances where they have obtained court injunctions to do so. Threatening you as a technique to get you into panic mode so that you can pay up is illegal.

9: Lie That They Represent the Company You Owe

Another trick that debt collectors use is to lie that they are direct representatives of the company you owe. They understand their limits as debt collectors, and would sometimes try to pretend that they are not debt collectors. This is illegal and you can report or sue them for this.

10: Provide False Credit Information to Credit Bureaus

If a debt collector is going to report you to a credit bureau, then he/she had better be sure you owe that debt and have the necessary evidence to back it up. If they do not, you can have them remove it from your credit report.

11: Send You False Court or Official Documents

Another tactic debt collectors and collection agencies use is that of sending you some official documents claiming they are court injunctions. They do this to get you to panic so that you can pay up very fast. Investigate any document they send you and if you discover that they are false, you can take legal actions against them.

12: Garnish the Following Assets after a Lawsuit

Even if a debt collector obtains a court injunction against you that allows them to forcefully collect their debts, they cannot touch some assets like:

1. Your social security benefits
2. Death and disability benefits
3. Military annuities and survivor's benefits
4. Veteran benefits
5. Student assistant
6. Civil service and federal retirement benefits
7. Disability benefits
8. Supplemental security income

13: Try to Collect Interest or Charges on the Debts

Lastly, debt collectors cannot charge interests, late payment charges, or other penalties on what you owe.

Let's now discuss how to report debt collection agencies for the above wrongdoings.

How to Report Debt Collection Agents for Harassment or Unfair Practices

If a debt collector is harassing you or has done any of the things not legally allowed by the Fair Debt Collection Practices Act, you should immediately inform them that the law in place keeps them from doing that, and inform them that you will be taking legal actions against them for it.

They will usually back off when you inform them that you will be suing them: no debt collector wants to "catch a case" for a $500 debt or have their businesses sanctioned for that. When you inform them that you will be suing them for malpractice or harassment, they will usually back off.

You could also take some other actions to show them that you are willing to walk the talk. You can:

- **Report them to the Consumer Financial Protection Bureau (CFPB)**

If the debt collector violates any of the FDCPA laws mentioned above, you can file a complaint against them with the Consumer Financial Protection Bureau (CFPB). Make sure you get the name of the debt collector and their company's names and report them to CFPB so that the bureau can impose legal sanctions against that debt collector.

- **Report them to the Federal Trade Commission**

You can also file a complaint against the debt collection agent with the Federal Trade Commission (FTC). FTC is an independent government agency that upholds debt collection laws and can take actions against erring debt collection agents.

- **Report them to The State Attorney General**

Some states have specific laws guiding debt collection. You can find out what your state's debt collection laws are; if it turns out that the debt collection agent has violated any of these laws, you can report them to the office of your state's attorney general so that the office can take legal actions against the debt collector.

- **Report to the Better Business Bureau**

Lastly, you can report the debt collection business or agency to the Better Business Bureau (BBB) to discourage businesses from using their services as debt collection agents.

With that in mind, let's now narrow the discussion down to when the debt collector plays by the rules. How do you deal with the situation? That's what we will be discussing next.

Chapter 3: What to Do When a Debt Collector Contacts You

Usually, many debt collectors will leave you alone when they find out that you are not willing to cooperate.

Debt collectors would rather spend their time and resources pursuing ignorant and fearful debtors than going after one who seems smart and ready to go toe to toe with them.

In addition, the costs of pursuing legal action are sometimes not worth it for debt collectors. Can you imagine taking a $200 debt case to court? It is not cost effective for them and is a waste of their time and resources and so, ***to beat debt collectors***, you must first ***show them that you fully understand debt collection laws and that you are not scared of going to court.*** Many of them will back off after this.

Your first line of defense against debt collection agents is to know how to respond to them, and how to communicate with them properly. You have to say the right things and respond the right way to avoid indicting yourself or saying the wrong things that the debt collector can use against you in a court of law.

Let us now discuss how to respond to debt collection agents when they call you up or send you a mail/letter requesting you make payments.

How to Respond to Debt Collection Agents on Phone

Here is how to respond to debt collectors who contact you via phone:

1: Always be Alert and Ask Smart Questions

Do not let them catch you off guard. You must always anticipate their calls and be ready to ask the right questions.

Sometimes, a debt collection agent may not have your current address; that means such a debt collection agent cannot send you any letters. That is one of the many ways to beat them at their game: because the law requires them to send you an official letter about what you owe within five days of contacting you.

If they do not have your address, there is no way to send this letter; however, if you let them catch you off-guard, they may cleverly sweet-talk you into giving them this information before you know what is happening. Therefore, you need to be 'uptight' when it comes to debt collection agents and avoid saying too much to them.

When they call, start by asking the following questions:

1. What is your name?

2. What is the name of the debt collection agency you represent?

3. What is the official address of the debt collection agency?

4. What is the name of the creditor?

5. How much does the creditor claim I owe? It is important to use the word 'claim' here because if you say something like "How much do I owe?" It means you are already agreeing up to the debt, something they can use against you in a court of law.

During this conversation, you want to get as much detail from the collector as possible while neglecting to give any information about yourself or your finances.

The debt collector may try to sound authoritative or use other intimidating or scare tactics to get you to give up more than you are willing to; think of a debt collector as a toothless dog because really, they cannot do anything to you except when the court orders it.

Record the Conversation

As soon as a debt collector calls and introduces him or herself, you should immediately inform the debt collector on the other end of the line that you will start recording the conversation and then press the record button on your phone to get all your conversation on record. If your phone does not come with the call-recording feature, you can buy a tape recorder and use it to record the calls instead— this means you have to put the phone on loudspeaker.

We have many innovative tape recorders that you can use to record phone conversations. The Olympus VN-7600PC is a very good product for this purpose; you can easily get it from online stores like Best Buy or Amazon for around $100.

You should also record any other conversations you have with the debt collector after that. If the debt collector leaves you a voicemail, make sure you keep a record of the voicemails sent to you. However, you must note that recording conversations on phone is illegal in some states so make sure you are aware of the position of the law on this in your state.

If it is illegal to record phone conversations in your state, avoid communicating with the debt collector on phone; instead, tell the debt collector to send you a letter instead. This will help you keep correspondences on the conversation in a legally acceptable way.

In states where it is illegal to record phone conversations, you can also use recorded voicemails in your defense.

Why You Should Record Your Conversations with a Debt Collector

Because any errors or misconduct—no matter how slight—by the debt collector can get you off the hook, and get your debt erased if the evidence is admitted in court. The law is not usually on the side of debt collectors who break the law while attempting to recover debts.

In the case of FOTI versus NCO FINANCIAL SYSTEMS INC., the court let the defendant off the hook because the debt collector failed to leave sufficient information that would help the defendant identify them as a debt collection agency.

Personally, I think that the defendant might have been avoiding the debt collector's calls and so the debt collector decided to leave him a series of voicemails and then took him to court after some time. However, once in court, the court ruled that there was no way the debtor could have known that NCO Financial Systems was a debt collection agency because the caller did not specifically use the word "debt collector or debt collection agency" in the voicemail left.

This is just one example of how keeping correspondences, especially phone calls and letters from debt collection agencies, can help your case against the debt collector.

Ask the Debt Collector to Send You an Official Letter

After asking the necessary questions, tell the debt collector to send you a letter to that effect. Tell them you really have no idea of the debt they are talking about, and that they should send you more details.

Now, this is one loophole: many debt collectors, especially debt buyers, do not have sufficient information about the debt you owe. Some will not even have your house address or know where to address the letter. There is a chance that they will want to get information from you especially your address. You should avoid giving it to them. You should simply tell them that since they claim you owe them, they should have all of this information in their records.

After you make this demand, the law mandates that the debt collector send you a debt validation letter within 5 days. The debt collector should then not contact you about the debt again until they have sent you this letter, and they must send the letter within 5 days.

SAMPLE PHONE CALL TRANSCRIPT TO USE WITH DEBT COLLECTORS

To make things super easy for you, I have come up with a sample phone call transcript you can use with debt collectors.

We shall outline two scripts you can use in different scenarios:

1st Script: If you are Not Sure about the Debt

Debt Collector: "Hello, can I speak to Charlie/ is this Charlie?"

Charlie: "Who am I speaking with please?"

NOTE: At this stage, the law states that the debt collector must identify himself or herself as a debt collection agent.

Debt Collector: "My name is Alex, a debt collector/collector from Dash Collections, the Collection agency representing Cups and Spoons Limited on your outstanding balance of $2,500. I need to know if you are ready to take care of the past due bill at this time."

Charlie: "Sir, "I'm going to be recording this conversation, please kindly hold on while I turn on my recording device."

NOTE: Use this pause to not only turn on your recorder, which you should do, but also take some time to ponder on the debt and try to remember if the statute of limitations on the debt has expired or otherwise- remember we talked about the statute of limitations earlier.

If you are unsure, return to the call.

Charlie: Ask the following questions so that you can get it on record:

1. What is your name?
2. What is the name of the debt collection agency you represent?

3. What is the official address of the debt collection agency?

4. What is the name of the creditor?

5. How much does the creditor claim I owe?

Charlie: "Please kindly confirm, are Cups and Spoons Limited your employer?"

NOTE: What you are trying to do here is to establish if the debt has been sold or handed over to a debt buyer/debt collection agency. Remember, I said earlier that the FDCPA laws do not apply to debt collectors employed directly by the creditor. Before you go ahead, you must establish that the caller is truly a debt collector. If the caller is a debt buyer and you do not wish to pay the debt, you can simply go on and say.

Charlie: "I am unable to communicate with debt collectors who are not employees or direct representatives of an acclaimed creditor. Please kindly give me your address so that I can send you a cease and desist letter in accordance with the FDCPA rules. I am also revoking any permission you have to call me at any number so please make this your last call to me."

2nd Script: If You Believe the Debt to Be an Error or Invalid

Debt Collector: "Hello, can I speak to Charlie/is this Charlie?"

Charlie: "Who am I speaking with please?"

NOTE: At this stage, the law states that the debt collector must identify himself or herself as a debt collection agent

Debt Collector: "My name is Alex, a debt collector/collector from Dash Collections, the Collection agency representing Cups and Spoons Limited on your outstanding balance of $2,500. I need to know if you are ready to take care of the past due bill at this time."

Charlie: "Sir, I'm going to be recording this conversation, please kindly hold on while I turn on my recording device."

This is not only a time to turn on your recorder, turn it on but also take some time to ponder on the debt and try to remember if the statute of limitations on the debt has expired or otherwise—we talked about the statute of limitations earlier.

If you are unsure, return to the call.

Charlie: "Ask the following questions so that you can get it on record:

1. What is your name?

2. What is the name of the debt collection agency you represent?

3. What is the official address of the debt collection agency?

4. What is the name of the creditor?

5. How much does the creditor claim I owe?

Charlie: "I strongly believe I do not owe this particular debt. You can send me information on the debt according to the FDCPA so that I can review it. I am also revoking any permission you have to call me at any number so please make this your last call to me."

Be aware that:

Debt collectors also have their own script for communicating with debtors. Many of them are smart and will already anticipate these responses from smart debtors so they will try to ask some questions in a bid to extend the communication and make you say things you should not say.

They usually have 'baits' in their script and mostly, they will ignore your responses and stick to their own script. You should ignore these baits and avoid saying anything else to them after you have verbally disputed the debt and requested an official letter.

The only question you can answer after this is to verify your address. You should only verify or tell them *"Yes please"* or *"No, that is not my address."*

At no point should you give the debt collector your current address even if they get it wrong?

If the debt collector calls you back, turn on the recording device again and say something along the lines of, "I already disputed this debt and revoked permission for further calls the last time you called. Therefore, this call is in violation of the FDCPA rules and you leave me no choice but to report this violation to the relevant authorities"

Terminate the call after this and then wait for the letter giving more information about the debt. When you receive their letter, send them a 'debt dispute' letter along with a 'cease and desist' letter.

Later chapters will have samples of these letters.

How to Respond to Letters or Mails

A debt collector may choose to send you a letter instead of calling you. It is also important to know how to handle these types of correspondences the right way.

Here are a few guidelines to help you respond to debt collector's letters correctly:

Never Call Back

Sometimes, a debt collector will offer vague information in their letters to you and then urge you to call back so that they can now interrogate you and use their tactics on you in a phone conversation. You should avoid calling them altogether; you should only respond to them via letters or mail as well.

Never provide any Information They Don't Already Have

If they do not have your address, do not give it to them. If they do not already have your phone number, do not give it to them. You should never give a debt collector any extra information about yourself, work, address, family, or anything else they do not already know.

Never Ignore Their Letters

Debt collection letters always come with a 30-day ultimatum after which the assumption is that you agree to the debt. It is important to reply to their letters as soon as you get it so that you can dispute the debt immediately.

Make sure you check the day of the letter postage to be sure that they left enough time to respond to the letter. If they only posted the letter 2 weeks before 30 days lapsed, then you can use that loophole against them in court.

Avoid Signing Documents from Debt Collection Agencies

Some debt collection agents will have no problem forging your signature on documents or tricking you to sign some documents. You should avoid signing documents from them. You can just write your name in full instead of signing documents.

Save Correspondences

Just as you would record conversations with debt collectors, you should save any copies of any letters you send to them or get from them.

Have Them Sign For Letters

Unscrupulous debt collectors can easily deny that they did not get your letters so make sure you use a reputable courier service that will have them sign for the letters so that you can keep evidence that they received your correspondences.

The procedure for dealing with debt collectors who send you letters is almost the same thing as dealing with those who choose to call you instead. You should immediately send them a letter to dispute the debt as well as a 'cease and desist' letter to stop them from contacting you about the debt.

If you do not owe the debt, know that the statute of limitation has passed, or do not wish to pay the debt, you should do the following:

❖ *First, you should send them a letter telling them to provide more information about the debt. Below a sample letter you can use below:*

Sample Letter Asking for More Information from the Debt Collector

[Your Name]

[Your Address] *Use the same address they sent the initial letter to you

[Date]

[Collector's Name]

[Collector's Company Name and Address]

Subject: Re: The same subject the collector used or the account number of the debt

Dear (Collector)

I am writing to you regarding the letter you sent me (or the call you made to my phone) on (Date) about a debt that you are trying to collect.

You identified the debt as xxxxx amount owed to xxxxxx creditor for xxxxxx purpose.

To enable me to review the said debt, please kindly provide the following information:

1. The name and address of the creditor

2. The amount owed

3. The account number used by the creditor

4. The original creditor and account number of the creditor (if the debt started with a different creditor).

5. The amount owed to the original creditor and its transference date.

6. Any other name by which I may be able to identify the original creditor if they have another name apart from their official name.

7. Whom the current creditor obtained the debt from, and when they obtained it.

8. Documentation and verification or agreement made with the creditor that created a valid requirement for the debt repayment.

9. If someone else incurred the debt, and I am now being required to pay the debt, please kindly provide valid documentation and verification as to why I am required to pay the debt.

I also need you to provide details about the amount and age of the debt. Please kindly provide the following details:

1. A copy of the last billing statement that was sent to me by the original creditor.

2. All additional charges or interest fees (if any) from the last billing statement. This should include an itemized list showing the dates and the amounts added.

3. Documentation and verification that the agreement that created the debt also authorized the addition of the interest, fees, and charges.

4. The date the creditor claims the debt fell due when it subsequently became delinquent.

5. The date when the last payment was made on the particular account.

6. Any charges or deductions on this account including details about how they were calculated and documentation or authorization to make these deductions or adjustments by the initial agreement that created the debt.

7. Evidence that the debt is actually within the statute of limitations

In addition to the above, I would like you to provide more details about the organization you represent before I can continue discussions about this debt with you. I will like to know:

1. If your debt collection agency is licensed to operate within xxxxx (your state) state

2. Name on the license, license number, and date

3. Name, address, and telephone number of the state that issued the license.

All of these will help me establish that you have the legal authority to collect this debt you claim I owe.

If you are licensed in a different state, please kindly provide evidence that your firm is licensed to operate in that state including details of the license issuing agency, name on the license, license number, and date, name, address and telephone number of the state that issued the license.

I need to hear from you as soon as possible to help me make an informed decision about this debt you claim I owe.

I am open to communicating with you about this matter; however in the meantime, please consider this debt as being in dispute and under discussion between us.

Thank you for your cooperation.

Kind regards,

[Your Name]

This letter requests information from debt collectors and on top to that, it helps scare scam or 'weak' debt collectors away because many of them usually do not have enough information or documentation to back up their claims.

Even the shrewdest of debt collectors is likely to turn 'jelly' after getting such a letter from a debtor because it means you know your rights, are ready to waste their time, not willing to pay, and cannot be intimidated.

❖ *If after you receive the requested letter from the debt collector, you are sure it is an error or that you do not owe the said debt, send another letter telling them that you do not owe the debt along with a 'cease and desist' order to stop them from communicating with you.*

Here is a sample letter to use:

SAMPLE DEBT DISPUTE WITH CEASE AND DESIST ORDER

[Your Name]

[Your Address] *Use the same address they sent the initial letter to you

[Date]

[Collector's Name]

[Collector's Company Name and Address]

Subject: Re: The same subject the collector used or the account number of the debt

Dear (Collector)

I am writing to you regarding the letter you sent me (or the call you made to my phone) on (Date) about a debt that you are trying to collect.

You identified the debt as xxxxx amount owed to xxxxxx creditor for xxxxxx purpose.

Having carefully reviewed the information you provided, I have concluded that I do not have any responsibility for the said debt.

Do not contact me about this debt anymore whether by phone, mail, letter, or any other platform or place.

If you decide to forward this debt to any other debt collection agency or report to any credit bureau or if you have already done so, I require you to report to them that this debt is disputed.

Thank you for your cooperation.

Yours sincerely,

[Your name]

❖ *If you do not wish to pay the debt or the statute of limitation has passed, send them a letter telling them to stop contacting you.*

Sample Cease and Desist Letter (If You Indeed Owe the Debt but Do Not Wish to Pay)

[Your Name]

[Your Address] *Use the same address they sent the initial letter to you

[Date]

[Collector's Name]

[Collector's Company Name and Address]

Subject: Re: The same subject the collector used or the account number of the debt

Dear (Collector)

I am writing to you regarding the letter you sent me (or the call you made to my phone) on (Date) about a debt that you are trying to collect.

You identified the debt as xxxxx amount owed to xxxxxx creditor for xxxxxx purpose.

Please cease all communication with me or this phone number/address about this debt.

Let it be on record that I dispute this debt and if you decide to report or have already reported this debt to any credit bureau, I require you to also report that this debt is disputed.

Thank you for your cooperation.

Yours sincerely,

[Your name]

❖ *If you have a lawyer and want them to deal with your lawyer instead (although the whole point of this book is so you can handle debt collectors yourself and save yourself some attorney fees), below is a sample letter to send:*

Sample Letter Directing a Debt Collector to Continue Communications with Your Lawyer

[Your Name]

[Your Address] *Use the same address they sent the initial letter to you

[Date]

[Collector's Name]

[Collector's Company Name and Address]

Subject: Re: The same subject the collector used or the account number of the debt

Dear (Collector),

I am writing to you regarding the letter you sent me (or the call you made to my phone) on (Date) about a debt that you are trying to collect.

You identified the debt as xxxxx amount owed to xxxxxx creditor for xxxxxx purpose.

Please do not contact me directly about this debt anymore. Direct all communications to my lawyer.

My lawyer's contact information is:

[Contact Information]

Thank you for your cooperation.

Yours sincerely,

[Your name]

WHAT TO DO AFTER A DEBT COLLECTOR CONTACTS YOU

After a debt collector calls/sends you a letter with further information about the said debt, it is important for you to take some steps so that in the event that the debt collector decides to take legal actions against you, you can have an advantage over them.

Here is what you should do:

Investigate the debt

Many debt collectors use fraudulent tactics: they try to intimidate you to pay money you do not owe and sometimes, the debt may be a case of identity theft, clerical errors, or any other errors. You should be sure what the case really is especially if you do not remember owing the debt the debt collector claims you owe.

Before you send your debt dispute letter, you should investigate the debt to be sure about what is really going on so that if the debt is an error, you can work on getting it removed from your credit report.

HOW TO INVESTIGATE A DEBT

To investigate the debt, you would have to:

Order Your Credit Report

We have three major credit-reporting bureaus; you are entitled to at least 2 copies of your credit report from these agencies yearly.

When you get notified about a debt especially one that you cannot remember or recognize, you should order your credit report and use it to trace the debt to see if you indeed owe what they claim you owe.

To get copies of your credit report, visit www.annualcreditreport.com.

Check Statute of Limitation

Next, you should confirm that the statute of limitation for the said debt has not passed. Check the date when the debt became delinquent, and find out what the statute of limitation for that type of debt is in your state to see if it has passed or not.

Reach out to the Creditor to Confirm

If you cannot find the said debt on your credit report and cannot remember the debt, there is a good chance that the debt collector is a fraud. Send a letter to the alleged creditor and request extensive information about the debts including when and how they were incurred, and the signed agreement between you and them. If the creditor fails to respond, you can cite this in court.

Dispute Errors in Your Credit Report

You have the right to dispute any errors on your credit report by contacting the credit bureau or hiring the services of a credit repair agency to help you remove the negative error from your credit report.

WHAT YOU SHOULD NEVER DO WHEN DEBT COLLECTORS CONTACT YOU

Now you already know what to do when a debt collector contacts you. There are also a few things you should avoid doing.

Many people, out of panic perhaps, take some steps that end up hurting their cases in court because they already did some things that looked like an admission of guilt.

When a debt collector contacts you about a debt, you should never:

Try to Hide Your Money or Assets

Do not try to hide your money or assets even if a debt collector threatens to garnish your bank account or assets. The law considers it illegal and fraudulent to hide your assets especially when you indeed owe the debt.

Apply for a New Line of Credit

The law also considers it fraudulent to abandon an old account and apply for a new line of credit when you are unable to pay what you owe other creditors.

Negotiate with them before Debt Validation

When a debt collector calls you about a debt, they do not expect you to know so much about the legal process and they are not expecting you to ask for debt validation documents; they will, therefore, try to get you to negotiate a settlement with them. Do not fall for this trap. If you want to negotiate, make sure you negotiate after you receive the debt validation documents.

STEPS TO TAKE IF A DEBT IS TRUE AND VALID

If you indeed owe the debt and the statute of limitation is yet to pass, then there are two options to take:

1: Negotiate an Offer to Pay a Paltry Sum

If you do not like the idea of being taken to court or reported to credit bureaus, then you can try to negotiate a settlement with the agency.

The truth is that debt collectors are willing to accept anything you offer them because they bought the debts from the original creditors for next to nothing so anything you offer them is still a profit for them. However, do not expect them to give in easily. Many of them will want to act tough and reject your offer.

If you use the tips I am about to give you, you will be able to negotiate with them successfully, and pay whatever you can afford.

How to Negotiate with Debt Collectors

You should:

Step 1: Decide How Much You Wish to Pay

You should offer to pay between 10-15% of the amount you owe and no more than that. Usually, they will try to get you to increase your offer; simply tell them that you cannot afford anything above that. They may also try to ask you questions about your assets, wages, and other personal questions. You do not have to answer any of these questions.

Step 2: Record the Negotiation Process

Debt collectors may negotiate with you and then after you have paid, they may do a double take and start claiming you negotiated with the wrong person and the person did not have the authority to make such decisions. All of this is in a bid to get you to part with some more money. Make sure you record the conversations (if your state allows it) or communicate via mail alone so that you can keep a record of the negotiation process.

Step 3: Negotiate a Full and Final Settlement

Make sure you always use the word "full and final settlement" when you are negotiating with debt collectors. Debt collectors are always fishing and looking for loopholes and therefore, when you negotiate with them and pay them off, they may come after you again claiming the money you paid was not in full and final settlement, and instead, was a part-payment and you still owe them.

When this happens, it becomes more difficult to win against them in court because making one payment means you already accept that you owe the debt and therefore, the law expects you to repay the debt.

Step 4: Ask for, and Sign a Debt Settlement Agreement Before You Make Payments

After negotiating with the debt collector, make sure you sign a debt settlement agreement with the debt collection agency before you make any payments so that they cannot come after you again in the future, and they cannot sell the debt to anyone else: they have to close the case after payment.

Step 5: Ask the Negative Report to be removed from Your Credit Report

If the debt has already been reported to a credit bureau, you must also negotiate with the debt collection agency to have the negative report removed from your credit report as one of the conditions for settlement.

Make sure this is also included in the debt settlement agreement you will co-sign with the debt collection agency. You should only make payments after the fulfillment of these conditions.

2: Call Their Bluff and See What Happens Next

If you call a collector's bluff by sending your cease and desist letter, the debt collector may decide to let you off the hook especially if what you owe is not worth going to court over.

However, the debt collector may decide to take any two courses of action:

1. Take you to court

2. Report to Credit Bureaus

The next chapter discusses how to handle the situation if the debt collector decides to take you to court.

Chapter 4: How to Beat a Debt Collection Agent in Court

One cool day, when sited at home or at work, you suddenly receive a certified letter from a law firm informing you that a debt collection agency is suing you for a debt you allegedly owe. It is normal to feel scared, feel bad, or have any other strong emotions about this situation because really, no one likes to have a court case.

There is no need to panic or let the situation intimidate you because this is what the debt collectors want: they want you to go into panic mode and probably call them up for a chance to settle the case out of court.

There is no need to do this either because as you are about to discover, there are numerous ways to outfox debt collectors and win against them in court after they sue you.

Follow the steps laid out in this chapter and there is a great chance that you will be able to win a debt collection case.

Step 1: Reply to the Summons

Many people choose to ignore the summons; this is wrong. As soon as you receive the letter, read it and look for important information within the letter.

Make sure you confirm that the letter is a genuine one since many desperate debt collectors often forge court summons. Confirm that the letter is an original.

Next, look at how many days you have to respond to the letter and state your readiness to defend yourself in court.

Reply to the letter stating your willingness to defend yourself immediately so that a date can be set for a hearing.

Please take note of that date and make sure you are in court on that day. If you do not show up, you lose the case by default and the court shall rule in favor of the collection company. This means you will now be compelled to pay the debt and the debt collector can garnish your wages or other allowable assets.

Step 2: Decide if You Need a Lawyer or Not

If the debt collector filed the case in a magisterial court, you can easily defend yourself using the defenses laid out later in this chapter. For higher courts though, you will need the services of a lawyer to defend you in court. However, you do not have to hire an expensive lawyer. You can hire an affordable one, prepare your defense using the tips in this book, and then hand it over to the lawyer.

Step 3: File a Request for Production

After responding to the summons, the next thing you need to do is to file a document called a "request for production."

This document is sent to the lawyer of the debt collection company and is simply a request that they provide you with a copy of the original agreement you made with the creditor with your signature on it.

The truth is that many debt collectors will not be able to produce this document because many creditors, utility companies, and credit card companies are bad record keepers.

Even when they have these records, it is sometimes very difficult for creditors to find these documents and give them to the debt collection company because it simply means that they will have to sift through thousands of documents to find this agreement.

The moment a creditor sells a debt to a debt buyer for a few pennies, they are done with that debt. They do not want their business activities disrupted by it so except in cases where the creditor operates a computerized file keeping system where it becomes easy to just pull out the records and give it to the debt collector to help their case, there is a significant chance that the debt collector will be unable to produce this document.

You file a request for production of the original contract you signed with the creditor by sending a letter that looks like this to the lawyer of the debt collector.

[Your Name]

[Your Address]

    [The Name of the Court]

[The Name of the Original Creditor] } Docket Number: [Insert]

[Plaintiff]	}	REQUEST FOR PRODUCTION
Versus	}	
[Your Name]	}	
[Defendant]	}	

The Defendant requests that the Plaintiff [Name of Original Creditor] produce the following documents in connection with this matter. In the event that objection is made, please state the reason for the objection. If denying the matter, please provide details about the reason why the answering party cannot provide the requested documents.

Please provide:

1. A copy of the application for credit signed by the defendant.

2. A copy of the initial executed contract in [name of original creditor]'s possession setting forth the terms that the defendant allegedly agreed to in connection with the credit.

3. If any modifications were made to the initial contract, kindly provide a copy of modification agreement allegedly signed by the defendant.

4. A copy of all statements, invoices, or receipts on the account from the inception till date.

5. Details regarding the alleged charges including how they were charged, reasons

for the charges, amount charged and the dates the charges were made.

6. Evidence of all payments received by the creditor on the account from the inception till date.

[Print date]

[Your Name]

[Your Signature]

CC: [Name of the Judge]

[Name of the Lawyer Representing the Creditor]

After writing this letter, print it, send a copy to the judge and another copy to the lawyer, and wait to see what happens.

What this letter does is warn the lawyer of the debt collection company that you are aware of your rights, that they do not have legal rights to the money they are trying to collect, and that you will be ready to go toe to toe with them in court.

Many debt collectors will drop the case at this point because they know that they do not have these documents. However, some will still like to proceed to court.

Step 4: Prepare Your Defense

Preparing your defense is all about looking for loopholes in the debt collector's case and methods that you can legally exploit to let yourself off the hook.

Here are a few defenses you can use against debt collectors in the court of law:

The Attachment Rule

In most states, the law requires that debt collectors or debt buyers must attach a copy of the written contract between the original creditor and debtor.

If the debt collector did not attach the document in their correspondences to you or in the letter sent you to inform you that they are suing you, you can file a motion in court requesting that they produce the document or that the case be dismissed if they cannot produce it.

Debt Limits for Law Suits

Find out what the minimum amount collectors are legally allowed to sue for in small claims courts within your state. Many states have limits for this and you can petition the court to dismiss the case if the amount you are being sued for does not fall within the limit.

Debt Validation

When the debt collector initially contacted you to inform you about the debt and you requested for more information about the debt, did they send it to you within the 5 days specified by the FDCPA law? If they did not, you can exploit this error and use against the debt collector in court.

"Accord and Satisfaction"

Another thing you can use in your defense is the debt satisfaction rule called "Accord and satisfaction."

Many utility companies and credit card companies usually take up insurance policies to protect their businesses from defaulters. If the original creditor has taken any compensation from insurance companies or has had a tax deduction for the loss their businesses incurred from the bad debt, then the loss is regarded as satisfied and the debt collector is not legally allowed to take you to court for a debt that has been satisfied.

Statute of Limitation

Find out what the statute of limitation for that type of debt is in your state. Be sure that the statute of limitation has not passed and if it has, you can bring this to the notice of the court and ask for a dismissal of the case.

"Scienti et Violenti nonfit Injuria"

In English, this translates to "An injury is not done to one who knows and wills it.

What this implies is that under the law, a person cannot make claims for damages or sue another person for it if they willingly and knowingly put themselves in harm's way.

Debt collectors are often aware that the debts they are inheriting are bad and delinquent debts, yet they go ahead to buy those debts thereby willfully putting themselves in harm's way.

You can cite this in court and ask the court to dismiss the case.

Statute of Frauds

A debt collection agent that is unable to produce an agreement you made with them (not the creditor this time) yet claim that you owe them, may be petitioned under the statute of fraud.

You entered into an agreement with the credit card company, utility company or whoever the creditor; you did not enter into an agreement with the collection agency and they did not provide any services to you and therefore, for them to claim that you owe them is fraudulent.

You can cite the statute of frauds in court to get the case dismissed.

Lack of Privity

A similar defense you can cite in court is "Lack of privity."

What this means is that when you were entering into a contract with the creditor, you did not enter into a contract with the debt collector. Therefore, and according to the Fair Debt Collection Practices Act that states that:

> *"The debt collector cannot collect any amount of money that is not authorized by the agreement creating the debt or permitted by the law because there is no agreement between the collector and the alleged debtor, no collection can be sustained",*
>
> ...no relationship exists between the plaintiff and the defendant, and the debt collection agency cannot collect any money not permitted or authorized by the agreement.

Meeting of the Minds

For a contract to be considered legally valid, there has to be something called "meeting of the minds".

Meeting of the minds represents a mutual agreement and a common understanding between the parties to the contract. The debt collection agency was not a party to the contract and there is no document to support the claims by the debt collector that there was a party to the contract between you and the original creditor at the inception when the contract was originally created. Therefore, no contract exists between the debt collection agency and the defendant, and you are under no obligation to pay them any money.

Failure of Consideration

If the debt collection agency is claiming that there is a valid contract with them, then where is the consideration? For a contract to be valid, there has to be something legally referred to as consideration.

Consideration means there must be an exchange of benefits between the parties entering into the contract. Since there was no exchange of goods or money between you and the debt collection agency, there is no consideration and therefore, no binding contract between you and the debt collection agency. In other words, you do not owe them any money.

Insufficient Specifity in the Pleading

In simple terms, this means that the debt collector must provide specific details about how the debts came to be. They need to specify:

1. What Goods or Services led to the debt?
2. How much and how frequently were the purchases or charges made to the debtor's account.

You can cite the debt collection law that states that:

"A defendant is entitled to know the dates on which individual transactions were made, the amounts, and the items purchased to be able to answer intelligently and determine what items he can admit and what items he can contest" Marine Bank, 25 pa. D. 7 C 3d at 267-69."

If the debt collector cannot provide sufficient information about the purchases made or services allegedly enjoyed, then they do not have enough facts about the debt to be able to come after you from a legal standpoint.

How to Start Your Defense in Court

On the day of the hearing, the first thing you should say in court is:

> *"Defendant is without information or sufficient knowledge to form an opinion as to the truth or accuracy of Plaintiff's claim, and based on that, denies generally and specifically the Plaintiff's claim."*

Here, you are referring to the fact that the debt collector has failed to provide all the documents you requested for and therefore, it is impossible for you to know if you actually owe the debt that they claim you do or not.

This is the first statement you should read out in court. After this, it is possible that the debt collector's lawyer will call you to the stands, place you under oath and then brandish some papers in your face asking if you deny signing 'this contract'.

Usually, what the lawyer is trying to do here is to trick you to admit to signing a contract with the creditor or debt collection agent since you are under oath and know the implication of lying under oath. However, and is usually the case, what the lawyer will be flashing before you is not the contract you signed but a decoy, an empty piece of paper because they usually do not have copies of the original contract from the creditor.

Regardless of what the debt collector's lawyer says, whether they indeed have the contract or not, as long as they did not send it to you at any point before the hearing date, just continue to stick to this statement

"Defendant is without information or sufficient knowledge to form an opinion............................"

Continue to repeat this no matter what the lawyer asks you about the contract or signed contract, the judge will lose his or her patience eventually and order the plaintiff to move on to other questions or sit down after which you may now move on to the other defenses discussed in this chapter.

Pick each one, read it to the judge, and remember to be confident and stick to your script no matter the level of intimidation or tricks used by the debt collector's lawyers.

I am certain that, using what you have learned in this guide, you shall be able to get yourself off the debt collector's hook without many hassles or spending too much. However, if you are not confident enough to defend yourself in court, consider hiring a lawyer and discussing these defenses with your lawyer so that he or she can know which loopholes to exploit to be able to get you off the hook.

Conclusion

We have come to the end of the book. Thank you for reading and congratulations on reading until the end.

With all the tips and guidelines laid out in this book, I have no doubt that you will be able to beat any debt collection agent at their game whether they decide to take you to court or not.

If the collection agency decides to report you to credit bureaus and hurt your credit score instead of taking you to court, you can take some steps to have your credit report repaired.

You can refer to my other book in the series to learn how to repair your credit.

If you found the book valuable, can you recommend it to others? One way to do that is to post a review on Amazon.

Please leave a review for this book on Amazon!

Thank you and good luck!

Printed in Great Britain
by Amazon